U.S. Withdrawal from the Antiballistic Missile Treaty

U.S. Withdrawal from the Antiballistic Missile Treaty

by Lynn F. Rusten

Center for the Study of Weapons of Mass Destruction
Case Study 2

Case Study Series Editors: Jeffrey A. Larsen and Erin R. Mahan

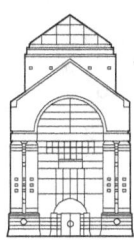

National Defense University Press
Washington, D.C.
January 2010

NDU Press publications are sold by the U.S. Government Printing Office. For ordering information, call (202) 512–1800 or write to the Superintendent of Documents, U.S. Government Printing Office, Washington, D.C. 20402. For the U.S. Government On-Line Bookstore go to: www.access.gpo.gov/su_docs/sale.html.

For current publications of the Institute for National Strategic Studies, consult the National Defense University Web site at: www.ndu.edu.

Contents

Setting the Stage: May 2001

We need new concepts of deterrence that rely on both offensive and defensive forces. Deterrence can no longer be based solely on the threat of nuclear retaliation. Defenses can strengthen deterrence by reducing the incentive for proliferation. We need a new framework that allows us to build missile defenses to counter the different threats of today's world. To do so, we must move beyond the constraints of the 30-year-old ABM Treaty. [1]

As President George W. Bush made these remarks in a speech at the National Defense University (NDU) on May 1, 2001, National Security Council (NSC) Senior Director for Proliferation Strategy, Counterproliferation, and Homeland Defense Robert Joseph listened attentively. Within just 4 months of taking office, President Bush was articulating one of his key national security priorities: setting the conditions for the United States to move full steam ahead on developing, testing, and eventually deploying a wide range of missile defense technologies and systems—a priority that in all likelihood would mean U.S. withdrawal from the 1972 Antiballistic Missile (ABM) Treaty. [2]

The ABM Treaty between the United States and the Soviet Union (and later Russia) barred both superpowers from deploying national defenses against long-range ballistic missiles and from building the foundation for such defenses. The treaty was based on the premise of mutual assured destruction, the belief that stability was ensured by each superpower having confidence in its ability to destroy the other, and the likelihood that if either power constructed a strategic defense, the other would build up its offensive nuclear forces to overwhelm it. The superpowers would therefore find themselves in a never-ending offensive-defensive arms race as each tried to assure the credibility of its offensive nuclear force. The treaty did, however, allow both sides to build defenses against short- and medium-range ballistic missiles. The ABM Treaty was negotiated and signed concurrently with the Interim Agreement on strategic offensive arms (commonly known as SALT I)—the first in what became a series of U.S.-Soviet strategic arms control agreements that first capped, and later reduced, the strategic nuclear arsenals of the two superpowers. [3] For this reason, both countries, when adversaries, considered the treaty a "cornerstone of strategic stability." But with the Cold War over, missile defense advocates, including Joseph, felt that the ABM Treaty's ban on nationwide missile defenses and its restraints on development and testing prevented the United States from developing and deploying defenses against the proliferating threat of ballistic missiles, especially from countries pursuing nuclear weapons capabilities and long-range missiles. [4]

In the months before the President delivered his NDU speech, Secretary of State Colin Powell was the most insistent among Bush's principal advisors that the President not make an abrupt announcement of U.S. withdrawal from the treaty without having laid the diplomatic groundwork for this decision. Powell advocated a gradual and deliberate approach to withdrawal that would be preceded by a process of diplomatic consultation. Secretary Powell's views emerged at a time when the United States was receiving considerable criticism at home and abroad for eschewing multilateralism and becoming too dismissive of international agreements and multilateral endeavors. Powell's perspective was based, in part, on the belief that the United States could conduct significant research and testing activities without bumping up against the ABM Treaty's constraints, and thus it was not necessary, as a programmatic matter, to withdraw from the treaty at that time. Or as John Bolton, the Under Secretary of State for Arms Control and International Security, more colorfully described Powell's views: "[The Department of] Defense had not progressed far enough operationally on missile defense for us to tank the ABM Treaty now."[5]

In drafting the President's NDU speech, Joseph listened carefully to Powell's wisdom about diplomatic consultations and made certain that the text placed greater emphasis on the administration's intention to begin consulting with U.S. allies, Russia, and China regarding the need for "a new framework that reflects a clear and clean break from the past, and especially from the adversarial legacy of the Cold War."[6] Even if these consultations might delay the final outcome, Joseph was confident that the United States was on a path to withdraw from the treaty—something that he and other missile defense advocates had been promoting for years. As Bolton later observed, "Whatever else we did, it was absolutely critical to get out of the ABM Treaty unambiguously. Then, whether we succeeded or failed in broader negotiations with Russia, we would be free to pursue a missile defense system to protect Americans from broader threats."[7]

National Security Council Decisionmaking Process

The National Security Council (NSC) was unusually swift and effective in reaching and implementing the decision to withdraw from the ABM Treaty. The process was tightly controlled by the NSC staff, ensuring that the decision was close-hold, shared with only a small, trusted group of people, and implemented in a short time. It reportedly began with the issuance in mid-February 2001—a mere 3 weeks after President Bush took office—of a National Security Presidential Directive that laid out the administration's conceptual framework for a new approach to deterrence and strategic offensive and defensive forces, including the intent to amend or withdraw from the ABM Treaty in order to deploy ballistic missile defenses and to reduce nuclear weapons to the lowest levels possible.[8] The directive was drafted by Joseph in the first few weeks of the administration. Subsequently, a small group of senior officials in the NSC, Office of the Vice President, Department of Defense, and Department of State met in April to discuss possible modalities of U.S. withdrawal from the treaty, given the President's campaign promise to proceed with deployment of a national missile defense and to conduct the missile defense testing that such a defense would require. Within days of that meeting, the NSC was circulating drafts of a Presidential speech for comment among that select group.[9]

Separately, the NSC tasked the Pentagon to review the U.S. nuclear posture to determine the levels to which the Nation could further reduce its strategic nuclear forces. This effort was overseen by Franklin Miller, the NSC Senior Director for Defense Policy and Arms Control, and it proceeded on a parallel track with the ABM Treaty withdrawal aspect of the new strategic framework.[10]

Historically, this was not the first time that a major national security decision was reached without conducting an extensive, comprehensive NSC-led interagency review of the rationale and consideration of alternative policy options. An iterative interagency process would have led to consideration of the issue at increasingly senior levels of government, leading ultimately to a Presidential decision, with all the ramifications of each option fully explored and conveyed to the President before he made his final decision.[11] In contrast, the process used in this case appears to have begun with the policy decision to deploy ballistic missile defenses already determined and codified from the top down in a Presidential decision directive. An administration backgrounder with a *New York Times* reporter intimated the fate of the ABM Treaty: "By issuing the directive, the official said, Mr. Bush will not declare his intention to withdraw from the Anti-Ballistic Missile Treaty, which the United States and Soviet Union signed in 1972 to prohibit national missile defenses. The review, however, appears intended to lay the foundation for a decision to do so in parallel with nuclear cutbacks."[12] In essence, the Presidential directive virtually foreclosed opportunity for dissent or reversal—especially from the State Department and its career bureaucracy, which was believed to be invested in the treaty in particular and the arms control process more generally.

With the decision to deploy ballistic missile defenses made and executed from the top down, the only issues for discussion were the details of implementation. Joseph was confident that the United States would eventually withdraw from the ABM Treaty; it was just a matter of when and in what diplomatic context the decision would be carried out. He believed the wisdom and effectiveness of this decisionmaking model for this particular issue was self-evident: he doubted whether the decision to withdraw would have been made if a more inclusive and deliberative interagency process had been used to resolve the question of how to permit the United States to proceed with missile defense testing, development, and deployment activities prohibited by the treaty. Joseph believed that the intentions of previous administrations had frequently been sabotaged and undercut by the bureaucratic process.[13]

Diplomacy on the New Strategic Framework: May–December 2001

Reflecting Secretary Powell's advice to conduct broad diplomatic consultations, the President's NDU speech contained the following commitments: "I've made it clear from the beginning that I would consult closely on the important subject with our friends and allies who are also threatened by missiles and weapons of mass destruction. . . . These will be real consultations. We are not presenting our friends and allies with unilateral decisions already made. We look forward to hearing their views, the views of our friends, and to take them into account."[14]

An intensive 7-month period of consultation and diplomacy ensued, with the objective of seeking the acquiescence of allies and countries such as Russia and China to a "new strategic framework" that the administration declared would include not only missile defenses, but also nonproliferation, counterproliferation, and unilateral nuclear reductions. At the time of the speech, the administration had not yet fully fleshed out its concept for that new framework, but its two main elements were the movement away from what it viewed as overreliance on legally binding agreements and the assurance that U.S. defense activities deemed necessary by the President would not be constrained. As John Bolton later put it, "In many respects . . . the 'new strategic framework' was still somewhat dreamy and academic, and debate within the administration focused on how to make it concrete and practical, both on the strategic offensive and defensive side of the equation."[15]

Immediately following the NDU speech, senior Bush administration officials, including Joseph, Deputy National Security Advisor Steve Hadley, Deputy Secretary of State Richard Armitage, and Deputy Secretary of Defense Paul Wolfowitz, were dispatched around the globe to consult with foreign capitals. Foreign leaders for the most part welcomed the consultations, but many European governments expressed concern about a potential unilateral withdrawal from the ABM Treaty. They also expressed their support not only for the treaty in particular, but also for arms control more broadly. The administration realized the consultation process would be protracted but felt confident that the allies would follow if Russia were on board with the United States.[16]

During President Bush's mid-June 2001 visit to Europe, Russian President Vladimir Putin, as well as key North Atlantic Treaty Organization (NATO) leaders, reiterated their concerns about U.S. plans and cautioned the United States against pushing ahead alone. A few days later,

Putin called for further consultations and hinted at his willingness to discuss modifying the ABM Treaty to permit the missile defense testing President Bush believed was necessary. In a 3-hour session with American news correspondents immediately after the summit, Putin said that "both the START [Strategic Arms Reduction Treaty] I and START II treaties would be negated by an American decision to build missile defenses in violation of the Antiballistic Missile Treaty of 1972." [17] But Powell and Secretary of Defense Donald Rumsfeld both dismissed the specter of a new arms race with Moscow, asserting that Russia must cut its arsenal because it could not afford to maintain its forces at current levels and that U.S. missile defenses would be limited, thus posing no threat to Russia's deterrent and removing any reason for Moscow to build up or alter its strategic forces.

At a July 2001 summit of the leaders of the Group of 8 industrialized nations in Genoa, Italy, a series of bilateral consultations began. A few days before the summit, Russian Foreign Minister Igor Ivanov[18] indicated readiness for a more intensive dialogue with the United States on the proposed new strategic framework, but he requested more clarity from the United States on its plans for a missile defense shield.[19]

At the summit, Presidents Bush and Putin agreed that the two nations would hold discussions on their offensive nuclear weapons and missile defenses and seek to reach agreement on a new strategic framework. Russian Defense Minister Sergei Ivanov indicated that he would recommend accepting modifications to the ABM Treaty if the resulting defenses would not undermine Russia's security. This acceptance would be in exchange for deep cuts in U.S. and Russian offensive forces. However, officials from the Bush administration, including the President himself, stated that the United States did not intend to participate in lengthy negotiations on formal arms control limits. They viewed these consultations as an opportunity for the United States to outline "both a new strategic framework for defensive weapons as well as the need to reduce offensive weapons."[20] Bolton characterized the Bush-Putin joint statement from Genoa as "disturbing" for the following reason: "It linked strategic offensive and defensive issues in a way that could allow Russia to condition elimination of the ABM Treaty on a new offensive weapons treaty. The linkage was unfortunate both because it reflected Cold War strategic thinking and because it could wrap the ABM Treaty withdrawal issue into endless arm[s] control negotiations, which we certainly did not want."[21]

More intensive U.S.-Russian consultations took place in August and September 2001. In a meeting billed as an "exchange of information," a Russian delegation received extensive briefings on U.S. technologies and plans for missile defense. Rumsfeld and Bolton traveled to Russia in mid-August in an unsuccessful attempt to convince Moscow that the two nations should withdraw from the ABM Treaty simultaneously. They did not engage in discussions about possible modifications to the ABM Treaty or in negotiations on reductions in offensive forces.[22] Bolton later recalled his impression of the meetings: "The Russians continued to reject both unilateral U.S. withdrawal and mutual withdrawal by jointly abrogating the ABM Treaty. I made it clear that we were open to other suggestions, but we would soon be announcing withdrawal, thus giving the Treaty's required six months' notice."[23] Russian officials complained that the two sides could not make progress in the negotiations because they still did not know what kind of missile defense the United States intended to build or how the U.S. missile defense program would be constrained by the ABM Treaty. This information was necessary to enable the two sides to devise amendments to relax the relevant constraints. The officials ruled out an early agreement on missile defenses and predicted that it could take a year or more for the parties to reach agreement on a framework to replace the ABM Treaty. Russia preferred to keep some form of treaty regime in place. While acknowledging that its relationship with the United States had changed, Russia nonetheless continued to regard offensive nuclear weapons as the central element of the U.S.-Russian strategic relationship and therefore continued to place a high value on the predictability offered by arms control agreements.[24]

Game Changer: September 11

The shocking and devastating al Qaeda terrorist attacks on the United States on September 11, 2001, completely altered the international context in which the negotiation on a new strategic framework was occurring. U.S. allies, as well as countries including Russia and China, were appalled by the attacks and genuinely sympathetic toward the United States. For the first time in its history, NATO invoked Article 5 of the Washington Treaty and committed to assist the United States. President Putin was the first international leader to call President Bush after the attacks and to offer his support. Russia shared its intelligence on and knowledge of Afghanistan with the United States and facilitated the use by U.S. forces of bases in the former Soviet republics to support the war against al Qaeda in Afghanistan. Deputy Minister of Foreign Affairs Georgi Mamedov, Bolton's Russian counterpart, told Bolton in a meeting on September 17, 2001, that the September 11 attacks "created a new window of opportunity in our relationship" and that "what is really important is that strong people unite in the face of tragedy."[25]

Speculation in the press that President Bush would inform President Putin in October of the U.S. intention to withdraw from the ABM Treaty proved wrong. After meeting on October 21 in Shanghai, Bush and Putin reported progress in their talks on missile defenses and nuclear force cuts, although they reached no agreements and remained divided over the ABM Treaty.

Nonetheless, at a joint press conference following their third face-to-face meeting, the two presidents sounded optimistic about being able to fashion a new U.S.-Russian strategic relationship. President Putin stated his belief that the two countries could "reach agreements," and Bush declared that both countries saw progress in their "efforts to build a new strategic framework." Yet their remarks revealed that they remained divided on the key issue of what to do about the ABM Treaty, which Bush described as "outdated" and "dangerous." He repeated his call for the two countries to "move beyond" the accord. Putin, on the other hand, said the treaty was "an important element of stability," although he again implied that Moscow was open to amending it.[26]

Bush framed most of his subsequent statements about the current relevance of the ABM Treaty in the context of the September 11 terrorist attacks. At one point he declared, "Both our nations must be able to defend ourselves against the new threats of the 21st century, including long-range ballistic missiles. The events of September the 11th make it clearer than ever that a Cold War ABM Treaty that prevents us from defending our people is outdated and, I believe, dangerous."[27]

Putin, who had joined Chinese President Jiang Zemin a day earlier in supporting the ABM Treaty, privately questioned Bush's reasoning and emphasis on rogue states, saying that "it would be difficult for me to agree that some terrorists will be able to capture intercontinental missiles and will be able to use them."[28]

Secretary Powell, who also traveled to Shanghai, underscored that President Bush had given neither a formal nor an informal notification of U.S. intent to withdraw from the ABM Treaty, adding, "We are under no constraints with respect to our thinking." He made clear that the key issue for the Bush administration was ensuring that the ABM Treaty did not limit U.S. missile defense testing. While emphasizing that Bush did not want the U.S. missile defense program to be "constrained artificially" by the treaty, Powell also noted that the administration was "looking at" Russian suggestions that the United States could "probably do more testing" than it thought it could under the treaty.[29] Although Powell had advocated that the administration modify its approach and negotiate an arrangement that would keep the ABM Treaty in place but provide greater flexibility for the United States to test and develop missile defenses, others in the administration, including Vice President Dick Cheney, Rumsfeld, Bolton, and Joseph, did not believe that outcome was possible. They viewed missile defense testing as literally "rocket science," therefore requiring a flexibility that even modifications to the ABM Treaty could not provide because the results of each test could not be anticipated. Bolton describes a Principals' meeting in July 2001:

Cheney said we should get out of the ABM Treaty "the sooner the better," and that we would end up with the worst of both worlds if we try to cut and trim it. Powell responded that Bush's program was to create a missile defense system, not simply to get out of the Treaty. He saw two options: withdrawal, or negotiating to modify or replace it. . . . Rumsfeld said we had to get out of the Treaty as soon as possible because its provisions were already restricting what we could do.[30]

Most significantly, Joseph and Miller each observed that Bush was strongly committed both to withdrawing from the ABM Treaty and to reducing U.S. nuclear forces unilaterally.[31]

Pre-Shanghai press reports had suggested that at that meeting, Bush would tell Putin the much anticipated level to which the United States would be willing to reduce its strategic offensive forces as part of the envisioned strategic framework and as a way to help win Russian acquiescence to U.S. missile defense plans. Yet in Shanghai, Bush reiterated an earlier pledge to reduce the deployed U.S. strategic arsenal but offered no specific number, explaining that the United States was still "analyzing" its nuclear arsenal. Putin stated in their joint news conference on October 21 that both sides reaffirmed their "mutual intention" to reduce strategic weapons. The task now, Putin commented, was to "develop parameters of such reductions and to design a reliable and verifiable method" for making the cuts. The Bush administration, however, had repeatedly insisted it had no interest in negotiated reductions, voicing a preference for unilateral, but parallel, reductions.[32]

National Security Advisor Condoleezza Rice downplayed the lack of any formal agreement at the Shanghai meeting and appeared to be lowering expectations for the upcoming Bush-Putin meeting in November. At her Shanghai press conference, Rice stated, "We're not looking for any specific breakthrough at any given meeting." She further remarked that the two sides would be working on U.S.-Russian strategic relations before, during, and after Putin's November visit, which would be split between Washington and Bush's Texas ranch.[33]

Meanwhile, Secretary Rumsfeld announced on October 25 that the Pentagon had decided against carrying out two October and November missile defense testing activities that he said could be viewed as violating the ABM Treaty. The cancellations seemed a goodwill gesture toward Russia that Washington would suspend activity that might violate the treaty while discussions with Moscow over its future continued. At the same time, the move suggested time was running short to reach an agreement on the treaty's future because the accord was impeding missile defense testing that the Pentagon wanted to conduct.[34]

Bush and Putin prepared for talks to be held in Washington and Crawford, Texas, in mid-November. Before traveling to the United States, Putin told U.S. journalists at a November 10 press conference that Moscow was ready to compromise and that a deal could be struck, but he said Russia first needed specific U.S. proposals. For example, with regard to the ABM Treaty, Putin asked, "What exactly [does the United States] want changed? What exactly hinders the implementation of the [missile defense] project devised by the U.S. administration?" Putin explained that Russia needed this type of information "in the practical proposals of our American partners." While commenting that he "partially" agreed with U.S. officials that the ABM Treaty was a Cold War relic, Defense Minister Ivanov said on November 3 that "before scrapping one agreement or another . . . we believe that this should be better done only after something has been created in the way of replacement." Ivanov's comment demonstrated why the two countries could not find common ground on missile defense: Moscow wanted to fashion the new U.S.-Russian relationship through treaties in which obligations and responsibilities were clearly spelled out and legally binding, whereas the Bush administration believed that such treaties were unnecessary between countries that were no longer enemies. At the same time, however, the Russian government realized that the Bush administration intended to withdraw from the ABM Treaty and wanted to make sure the exit was choreographed so that it was not an issue in their relationship.[35]

During 3 days of talks, Bush and Putin failed to reach an agreement that would permit the United States to move forward with its missile defense plans. Despite a growing rapport between the two presidents, and parallel pledges by each of them to cut their deployed strategic nuclear forces by roughly two-thirds, they were unable to narrow their differences over how to reconcile U.S. pursuit of nationwide strategic ballistic missile defenses with the 1972 ABM Treaty, which prohibited such defenses. The Bush administration made clear that it preferred unilateral or joint withdrawal from the treaty in order to pursue missile defenses unfettered, whereas Russia wanted to preserve the accord or at least keep in place some limits on future strategic missile defenses.[36]

During a question-and-answer session at a Crawford school, Putin told the audience, "We differ in the ways and means" of addressing future threats. Yet the U.S. side downplayed the differences, contending that the U.S.-Russian relationship could not be undermined by a dispute over a single issue. Bush declared, "Our disagreements will not divide us."[37] Rice told reporters on November 15 that the missile defense issue was "a smaller element of the U.S.-Russia relationship than it was several months ago" and that it was "not going to have an effect on the relationship as a whole."[38]

Although speculation had existed before the summit that Russia might agree to a deal to modify or suspend the ABM Treaty's prohibitions on testing sea- and air-based components of strategic defenses to forestall a possible U.S. withdrawal from the accord, no such agreement was concluded. The presidents, however, pledged to continue their discussions, and Putin sounded confident about the possibility of reaching an agreement: "One can rest assured that whatever final solution is found, it will not threaten . . . the interests of both our countries and of the world."[39]

Withdrawal Announcement

On December 13, 2001, Bush formally announced the intention of the United States to withdraw from the ABM Treaty. According to the treaty's own terms, the withdrawal would take effect 6 months after the date of notification. Bush had privately informed Putin in November that the United States would make the official announcement in December.[40] Thus, the policy objective set forth by the February National Security Presidential Directive and the President's May 2001 NDU speech was achieved, after 10 months of preparing the way diplomatically with Russia.

In the days before Bush's announcement, the White House called Putin in an effort to craft statements that would indicate the withdrawal would not upset the bilateral relationship. In a televised address to the Russian nation, Putin called the U.S. decision to withdraw from the treaty "mistaken," but added that "the decision taken by the United States does not pose a threat to the national security of the Russian Federation"—an announcement that administration officials considered enormously significant. They were further heartened by Putin's declaration 2 days earlier of Russia's commitment to reach an accord on strategic arms reduction.[41]

Epilogue

Moscow Treaty Negotiations

Although Bush had initially insisted that the United States and Russia should move away from formal arms control treaties and reduce nuclear forces unilaterally or in parallel, the United States did eventually agree, as a concession to Russia in the context of ABM Treaty withdrawal and also because Bush was personally committed to offensive force reductions, to codify further nuclear reductions in a short, legally binding agreement. At their meeting in July 2001, Presidents Bush and Putin had decided that the two nations would begin consultations on offensive and defensive weapons. But the talks on nuclear reductions made little progress for several months, with Russia complaining that the United States had not outlined any specific proposals for deep reductions, and the Bush administration responding that the Defense Department had not completed its review of the U.S. nuclear force posture. Miller recalled that it took several months for the Pentagon to complete its nuclear posture review and for the administration to settle on specific numbers for a reduced U.S. nuclear force. In the end, Washington settled on a range of 1,700 to 2,200 operationally deployed warheads, although some, including Miller, supported somewhat lower levels. The State Department did not play a significant role in determining the U.S. position on reductions.[42]

Following the terrorist attacks of September 11 and only a few months prior to his announcement on ABM Treaty withdrawal, President Bush, who was philosophically committed to strategic reductions—although not necessarily to codifying them in arms control treaties—became personally dedicated to the idea of reaching an agreement with Russia on reductions in parallel with the U.S. withdrawal from the ABM Treaty. As Bolton observed regarding the Bush-Putin meeting in Shanghai on October 17, 2001, "Bush returned from Shanghai determined to decide the issue of offensive numbers, and Powell had the distinct impression Bush wanted a treaty to announce in spring 2002."[43] According to Bolton, while Powell and Rice were advocates of an agreement on strategic offensive forces, Cheney, Rumsfeld, and he disagreed: "Powell told me Cheney was grumbling about the whole direction he and Rice were taking, and Rumsfeld felt the same way. It was certainly the way I felt."[44] But Bush had made up his mind.

On November 13, 2001, Bush announced that the United States would reduce the number of operationally deployed warheads on strategic offensive nuclear weapons to between 1,700 and 2,200 over 10 years. Putin indicated Russia was prepared to reduce its forces even lower, to 1,500, but continued to press for codification of the reductions in a legally binding treaty that included verification measures.[45]

The two sides intensified their discussions in January 2002, after the United States announced its intent to withdraw. In a notable concession to Russia, Secretary Powell told Congress in early February that the United States would be willing to sign a "legally binding" document on nuclear reductions. Russian officials praised the change in the U.S. position, but the sides remained at odds over the content of the agreement. Russia continued to insist that it include legally binding limits on nuclear warheads, with strict counting rules and formal elimination procedures, while the United States preferred a less formal declaration of intended reductions, with provisions for transparency to confirm the number of deployed warheads.

At a February 12 Principals Committee meeting, Bush decided to agree to a legally binding treaty, overruling Cheney and Rumsfeld. Bush was persuaded by the case Putin made to him about his need to have a treaty on offensive reductions to mitigate the sting of U.S. withdrawal from the ABM Treaty. In his memoirs, Bolton recounts Bush's decision:

After hearing everyone out, Bush said: "I believe we must have something that lasts beyond our presidencies. The strategic relationship with Russia is something that's important for the next ten years. So, to cement relations, I'm willing to throw the guy [Putin] some bones." Bush related to Putin's own domestic political vulnerability, since he "is on thin ice in his own mind. I want to give him a document he can hold up," to help Putin "bring her [Russia] West. I view this paper, frankly, as part of the larger strategy to link Russia with us. We need a document that he can hold up and say, 'Time is on our side' in May."[46]

In March, Bush stated that the parties should seek a formal agreement that would "outlive both of us," and suggested the agreement should include measures for transparency. After a meeting in April 2002, Powell was reportedly "pleased with the progress" made during the talks, even though the sides remained at odds over the means they would use to count warheads and monitor reductions under the new agreement. Whereas Russia preferred to maximize the predictability and irreversibility of the reductions, the United States sought to maximize flexibility in how it would implement the reductions and configure its nuclear forces. Finally, in mid-May, Bush announced that an agreement had been reached.

Bush and Putin signed the new Strategic Offensive Reductions Treaty (SORT) on May 24, 2002. The treaty would require each side to reduce its "strategic nuclear warheads" within the range of 1,700 to 2,200 by the year 2012. The three-page document contained no counting rules or verification provisions, but was negotiated with the expectation that START I, with its robust verification provisions, would remain in force concurrently, and that additional transparency measures would be worked out subsequently, thus facilitating verification of SORT. Miller noted, however, that significant administration efforts to get the U.S. interagency community to agree on a set of further transparency measures and to negotiate them with Russia were ultimately unsuccessful. This was, in part, because Iraq War planning and execution came to dominate the attention of the national security principals in the administration. Nor did the administration ever propose to Russia a follow-on set of nuclear reductions, which Miller believed had been a genuine goal of Bush.

Russia's Reaction to Withdrawal

Little pageantry or protest marked the U.S. move abrogating the ABM Treaty and its prohibition against nationwide missile defenses, despite often fierce debate on the accord within Washington and around the world. Bush issued a short written statement on June 13, 2002, the day the treaty expired, in which he noted that it was "now behind us," and he reiterated his commitment to deploy missile defenses "as soon as possible" to protect against "growing missile threats."[47]

The President's subdued commemoration of the treaty's passing contrasted sharply with his administration's earlier fervent attacks on the accord. The Russian reaction was also muted. By this time, the United States and Russia had negotiated SORT and signed a joint declaration outlining a new framework for mutual cooperation. Although some tensions remained in the U.S.-Russia relationship, particularly with respect to Russia's nuclear cooperation with Iran, cooperation continued to grow. The U.S. withdrawal from the ABM Treaty no longer seemed the cataclysmic event some feared. Foreign Minister Igor Ivanov noted the event, but stated the "the primary aim now is to minimize the negative consequences of the U.S. withdrawal" and concentrate on offensive reductions.[48] He and other Russian officials believed that Russia had convinced the United States to continue negotiations on reductions in strategic offensive forces, which represented a significant achievement for Russian diplomacy. Furthermore, Defense Minister Sergei Ivanov noted that the U.S. missile defense system did not yet exist and, therefore, there was no reason for Russia to retaliate.[49] However, Russia did announce the next day that it would no longer be bound by START II, a move that was largely symbolic, given that START II never entered into force and that it was effectively superseded by SORT.

In the wake of September 11, 2001, Putin apparently did not want to jeopardize warming relations with Washington by unduly lamenting an action to which the Bush administration was dedicated and that could not be undone. Speaking the day of the U.S. withdrawal, Foreign Minister Ivanov said that Russia regretted the action but that it was "now a fait accompli" and "it is our task to minimize the adverse consequences."[50]

On June 13, 2002, the U.S. withdrawal from the ABM Treaty became effective. In July 2004, the first operational ballistic missile interceptor for a national missile defense system was installed at Fort Greely, Alaska.[51]

Notes

[1] George W. Bush, "Remarks at the National Defense University, May 1, 2001," *Public Papers of the Presidents: George W. Bush*, 2001, vol. 1 (Washington, DC: U.S. Government Printing Office), 470–473.

[2] Author interview with Robert Joseph, Senior Director for Proliferation Strategy, Counterproliferation, and Homeland Defense, National Security Council (2001–2005), and Under Secretary for Arms Control and International Security, Department of State (2005–2007), May 4, 2009.

[3] Full texts of the Anti-Ballistic Missile Treaty and the Interim Agreement between the United States of America and the Union of Soviet Socialist Republics on Certain Measures with Respect to the Limitation of Strategic Offensive Arms are in *Documents on Disarmament* (Washington, DC: U.S. Arms Control and Disarmament Agency, 1990), 157–161 and 169–176.

[4] The George W. Bush administration had inherited an ABM Treaty–compliant national and theater missile defense (TMD) program from the Bill Clinton administration. The programs under way for national missile defense included research and development (not deployment) of ground-based midcourse ballistic missile defense interceptor missiles and their associated radar and tracking upgrades. The programs under way for TMD included seabased ballistic missile defenses (Aegis), tactical missiles for point defense against descending missile warheads (the Theater High-Altitude Area Defense program and the Patriot Advanced Capability missile), and research on airborne laser platforms to attack missiles during their boost phase. The Bush administration wanted to eliminate the distinction between national and theater missile defense programs (inherent in the ABM Treaty and associated agreements on ABM–TMD demarcation reached during the Clinton era) and proceed with deployment of a limited national missile defense (sized for a threat posed by small, hostile states such as North Korea), which it viewed as the centerpiece of its new strategic framework. See Jeffrey A. Larsen and Kerry M. Kartchner, *Emerging Missile Challenges and Improving Active Defenses*, Counterproliferation Papers, Future Warfare Series No. 25 (Maxwell Air Force Base, AL: United States Air Force Counterproliferation Center, August 2004); "Factfile: U.S. Missile Defense Programs at a Glance," *Arms Control Today*, June 2003, 20–28; "The President Discusses National Missile Defense," White House Web site, December 12, 2001, available at <www.whitehouse.gov/news/releases/2001/12/20011213-4.html>; and Philip E. Coyle, "Rhetoric or Reality? Missile Defense Under Bush," *Arms Control Today*, May 2002.

[5] John Bolton, *Surrender Is Not an Option* (New York: Threshold Books, 2007), 57; for additional insight into Powell's views, see Mary Dejevsky, "Powell: U.S. Not About to Ditch Treaty on Defences," *The Independent* (London), June 18, 2001, 12; and Barbara Slavin et al., "Powell Reflects on 6 Months as Secretary of State," *USA Today*, July 17, 2001, 10A.

[6] Bush.

[7] Bolton, 56.

[8] As reported by Steven Lee Myers, "Bush in First Steps to Shrink Arsenal of U.S. Warheads," *The New York Times*, February 9, 2001.

[9] Author interview with Joseph.

[10] Author interview with Franklin C. Miller, Senior Director for Defense Policy and Arms Control, National Security Council (2001–2005), June 8, 2009.

[11] For first-hand perspectives from former National Security Council principals on the formulation of arms control policy across Presidential administrations, see Ivo H. Daalder and I.M. Destler, moderators, "Arms Control Policy and the National Security Council," *The National Security Council Project: Oral History Roundtables*, March 23, 2000 (Washington, DC: Center for International and Security Studies at Maryland and Brookings Institution, 2000), 1–61.

[12] Myers.

[13] Author interview with Joseph.

[14] Bush.

[15] Bolton, 55.

[16] "Missile Defense Consultations Abroad Yield Little Progress," *Arms Control Today*, June 2001; see author interview with Joseph for insight into the Russian position.

[17] Patrick Tyler, "Putin Says Russia Would Add Arms to Counter Shield," *The New York Times*, June 19, 2001, A1.

[18] Not to be confused with Russian Defense Minister Sergei Ivanov, widely regarded as Putin's closest advisor on strategic affairs.

[19] "Russian Foreign Minister Says 'No Bargaining' with U.S. on Strategic Issues," BBC Worldwide Monitoring, July 18, 2001. Ivanov declared that "we will be ready to begin concrete discussions on this issue as soon as the U.S. side displays its willingness. . . . Without clearness in general approaches, it hardly makes sense to draw conclusions on individual aspects of this problem."

[20] "The President's News Conference with President Vladimir Putin of Russia in Genoa, July 22, 2001," in *Public Papers of the Presidents: George W. Bush*, 2001, vol. 2, 891–892. For an analysis, see "U.S.-Russian Differences Remain on Missile Defenses, ABM Treaty," *Arms Control Today*, September 2001.

[21] Bolton, 63.

[22] Ari Fleischer, White House briefing, August 22, 2001.

[23] Bolton, 66.

[24] Amy Woolf, "Nuclear Arms Control: The U.S.-Russian Agenda," Congressional Research Service Issue Brief for Congress, updated September 22, 2003; Woolf, "National Missile Defense: Russia's Reaction," Congressional Research Service Report for Congress, updated June 14, 2002.

[25] Bolton, 67.

[26] "The President's News Conference with President Vladimir Putin of Russia in Shanghai," *Public Papers of the Presidents: George W. Bush*, 2001, vol. 2, 1287–1291.

[27] Ibid., 1288.

[28] Quoted in "U.S., Russia Still Seeking Common Ground on Missile Defense," *Arms Control Today*, November 2001.

[29] Ibid. For additional insight into Powell's views on the ABM Treaty, see Bill Keller, "The World According to Powell," *The New York Times*, November 25, 2001.

[30] Bolton, 61.

[31] Author interviews with Joseph and Miller.

[32] "The President's News Conference with President Vladimir Putin of Russia in Shanghai, October 21, 2001," in *Public Papers of the Presidents: George W. Bush*, 2001, vol. 2, 1287–1291. See also "U.S., Russia Still Seeking Common Ground on Missile Defense."

[33] "U.S., Russia Still Seeking Common Ground on Missile Defense."

[34] "U.S. Cancels Missile Test to Repay Ally Putin," *The Times* (London), October 26, 2001.

[35] "No Bush-Putin Agreement on ABM Fate and Missile Defenses," *Arms Control Today*, December 2001.

[36] "Joint Statement by President George W. Bush and President Vladimir V. Putin of Russia, November 13, 2001," *Public Papers of the Presidents: George W. Bush*, 2001, vol. 2, 1399–1400, and "Remarks on Arrival in Waco, Texas, and an Exchange with Reporters, November 13, 2001," 1404–1405.

[37] "Remarks with President Vladimir Putin of Russia and Question and Answer Period with Crawford High School Students in Crawford, November 15, 2001," *Public Papers of the Presidents: George W. Bush*, 2001, vol. 2, 1409–1418.

[38] "No Bush-Putin Agreement on ABM Fate and Missile Defenses," *Arms Control Today*, December 2001.

[39] "Remarks with President Vladimir Putin of Russia and Question and Answer Period with Crawford High School Students in Crawford."

[40] Bolton, 74.

[41] Author interview with Joseph. See also "Russia and U.S. to Make Arms Cut," *The Times* (London), December 11, 2001.

[42] Author interview with Miller.

[43] Bolton, 69.

[44] Ibid., 69–70.

[45] Woolf, "Nuclear Arms Control: The U.S.-Russian Agenda."

[46] Bolton, 77.

[47] "U.S. Withdraws from ABM Treaty; Global Response Muted," *Arms Control Today*, July 2002.

[48] Amy Woolf, "National Missile Defense: Russia's Reaction," Congressional Research Service Report for Congress, updated June 14, 2002.

[49] Ibid.

[50] Ibid.

[51] Frances FitzGerald, "Indefensible," *The New Yorker*, October 4, 2004.

About the Author

Lynn F. Rusten was an independent consultant when she wrote this case study. Since August 2009, she has been the Director for Strategic Planning in the Bureau of Verification, Compliance, and Implementation at the U.S. Department of State. In that capacity, she provides policy support to the negotiations with the Russian Federation on a Strategic Arms Reduction Treaty (START) follow-on and leads planning efforts related to future nuclear arms reduction negotiations and strategic dialogues with other nuclear powers. From 2003 to 2008, she was a senior professional staff member on the Senate Armed Services Committee, handling a wide range of foreign and defense policy issues.

Ms. Rusten previously served in the executive branch from 1991 to 2002, including on the Secretary of State's Policy Planning Staff, where she advised department principals on arms control and nonproliferation policies, relations with Europe and Russia, and political-military affairs. At State and the U.S. Arms Control and Disarmament Agency, she worked on strategic arms control policy and treaty negotiation and implementation, serving as an advisor on the U.S. START delegation and chairing interagency working groups charged with negotiating and implementing the START and Intermediate-range Nuclear Forces Treaties.

Ms. Rusten received an M.S. in National Security Strategy from the National War College, an M.A. in Russian and East European Studies from the University of Michigan, and a B.A. in Government with High Honors from Oberlin College.

For additional information, including publication requests, please contact the Center directly at
WMDWebmaster@ndu.edu or (202) 433–6343 or visit the Center Web site at
www.ndu.edu/wmdcenter/index.cfm